A
Masterpiece
for
Bess

A Masterpiece for Bess

WRITTEN BY
LARA BERGEN

ILLUSTRATED BY
THE DISNEY STORYBOOK ARTISTS

HarperCollins *Children's Books*

First published in the USA by Disney Press,
114 Fifth Avenue, New York, New York, 10011-5690.

First published in Great Britain in 2006
by HarperCollins Children's Books.
HarperCollins Children's Books is a division of
HarperCollins Publishers,
77 - 85 Fulham Palace Road, Hammersmith, London, W6 8JB.

The HarperCollins Children's Books website is
www.harpercollinschildrensbooks.co.uk

978-0-00-721401-3
0-00-721401-4

1

Printed and bound in the UK

Visit disneyfairies.com

This book is proudly printed on paper which contains wood
from well managed forests, certified in accordance with
the rules of the Forest Stewardship Council.
For more information about FSC,
please visit www.fsc-uk.org

Mixed Sources
Product group from well-managed
forests and other controlled sources
www.fsc.org Cert no. SW-COC-1806
© 1996 Forest Stewardship Council
FSC

All About Fairies

IF YOU HEAD toward the second star on your right and fly straight on till morning, you'll come to Never Land, a magical island where mermaids play and children never grow up.

When you arrive, you might hear something like the tinkling of little bells. Follow that sound and you'll find Pixie Hollow, the secret heart of Never Land.

A great old maple tree grows in Pixie Hollow, and in it live hundreds of fairies and sparrow men. Some of them can do water magic, others can fly like the wind, and still others can speak to animals. You see, Pixie Hollow is the Never fairies' kingdom, and each fairy who lives there has a special, extraordinary talent.

Not far from the Home Tree, nestled in the branches of a hawthorn, is Mother Dove, the most magical creature of all. She sits on her egg, watching over the fairies, who in turn watch over her. For as long as Mother Dove's egg stays well and whole, no one in Never Land will ever grow old.

Once, Mother Dove's egg *was* broken. But we are not telling the story of the egg here. Now it is time for Bess's tale...

A
Masterpiece
for
Bess

"EVERYBODY! COME TO my room!"

Tinker Bell flew about the tearoom. In a silvery voice she called out to the fairies and sparrow men gathered around the tables.

Lily and Rosetta, two garden-talent fairies, looked up from their breakfast of elderberry scones.

"What's the hurry, Tink?" asked Lily.

"Bess has just painted my portrait –

and you've got to come and see it!" Tinker Bell urged.

Rosetta and Lily looked at each other in surprise. It wasn't every day that Bess painted a new portrait! What was the occasion? they wondered. But before they could ask, Tink had darted out the tearoom door and into the kitchen.

"Let's go," Rosetta said to Lily. They followed Tink through the Home Tree up to her room.

There the fairies packed themselves in wing to wing, like honeybees in a hive. They could see Bess, in her usual paint splattered skirt, standing at the front of the room. She was hanging a life-size, five-inch painting of Tinker Bell.

"Isn't it amazing?" gushed Tink. She flew up behind Lily and Rosetta and landed with a bounce on her loaf-pan bed.

And indeed it was. Bess's painting was so lifelike, if a fairy hadn't known better, she might have thought there were *two* Tinks in the room. No detail – from the dimples in Tink's cheeks to her woven sweetgrass belt – was overlooked. What Tink loved most about the painting, though, were the gleaming metal objects piled all around her: pots, pans, kettles, and colanders. She felt as if she could almost pull each one out of the painting.

It was a perfect portrait, as everyone could see. Right away the oohs and aahs began to echo off the tin walls of Tink's room.

"It's lovely!" said Lily. "Bess, you've outdone yourself again!"

"You're too kind. Really," Bess said.

Her lemon yellow glow turned slightly tangerine as she blushed. As Pixie Hollow's busiest painter, she was used to praise. But she never tired of hearing it.

"It's just what Tink's room needed," added Gwinn, a decoration-talent fairy. She gazed around Tink's metal-filled room.

"What's the occasion?" asked Rosetta.

"Oh, no occasion, really," said Bess. She brushed her long brown bangs out of her violet eyes. "Tink fixed my best palette knife, and I wanted to do something nice in return."

All around her, the fairies murmured approvingly. Bess felt her heart swell with pride. *This is what art is all about,* she thought. Times like these made her work worthwhile.

"Personally, I don't see what the fuss is for," a thorny voice said above the din. "Honestly, my little darlings, what's so great about a fairy standing still?"

Bess didn't have to turn around. She knew who the voice belonged to – and so did everybody else. Vidia, the fastest – and by far the meanest – of the fast-flying-talent fairies, came forward.

"Oh, Vidia," Tink said with a groan. "You wouldn't know fine art if it flew up and nipped you on the nose."

"Yeah, don't listen to her, Bess," Gwinn called out.

"It's okay," Bess assured them. "Every fairy is welcome to have her own opinion."

But as she looked at the portrait again,

she frowned slightly. It wasn't that Vidia's criticism bothered her. She'd learned long ago to let the spiteful fairy's snide comments roll off her wings like dewdrops. But Vidia's remark had started the wheels in Bess's mind turning.

"You know… ," Bess began.

She searched the room for Vidia. But the fairy had already flown away.

"'You know' what?" asked Tink.

Bess shook her head. She turned to Tink with a sunny grin. "There's a whole day ahead of us!" she said. "I don't know about you fairies, but I've got work to do."

Spreading her wings, she lifted into the air. "Thanks for coming, everyone," she called.

And with a happy wave, Bess zipped off to her studio.

2

NOWHERE ELSE DID Bess feel as content as she did in her studio.

Most of the art-talent fairies had studios in the lower branches of the Home Tree. But to Bess there never seemed to be quite enough light – or privacy – there to get her work done. Instead, she had made her studio in an old wooden tangerine crate that had washed up onto a shore of Never Land. She had moved the crate (using magic, of course) to the sunniest, most peaceful corner of Pixie Hollow. It had been her home away from home ever since.

Over time, she'd added things to the crate: a birch-bark cabinet to keep her canvases dry, a soapstone sink in which to wash her brushes, and even a twig cot with a thick hummingbird-down quilt to sleep on when she was painting late into the night.

Bess's studio had grown more and more cluttered. It was, in fact, a bit of a mess. She was not one for tidying up. Why put things away, she always wondered, when you were sure to have to pull them out again someday?

As soon as she reached her studio, Bess began to mix her paints. She took a jar of fragrant linseed oil down from a shelf. Next she brought out a gleaming cherrywood box. The box was polished to a mirrorlike shine. Bess's name was carved into the lid. A carpenter-talent fairy had given it to her as a gift many years before. It was still one of her most prized possessions.

Bess lifted the top of the box. She looked down at the rainbow of powdered pigments inside. Of all the things in her studio, these were the ones she treated like gold.

"Hmm," she mused out loud. "Which colours should I mix first? Orange? Indigo? Hmm... What is that *smell*?"

Following her nose, Bess turned to find two brown eyes peeking in at her through the slats in the tangerine crate.

"Dulcie?" she said in suprise. "Is that you?"

Visitors to her studio were rare. Bess fumbled with the latch as she opened the door. "What is it?"

"Oh, nothing," said Dulcie sweetly.

"I was just passing through the orchard and thought I'd say hi. Oh! And I thought you might like some poppy puff rolls. Fresh out of the oven!"

Dulcie grinned and held up a basket. She lifted a checked linen cloth off the top. The rich scents of butter and tarragon filled Bess's nose. Her mouth began to water.

"Goodness, Dulcie – your famous rolls. You're really too kind!" said Bess, more surprised than ever.

"I thought you'd be hungry," said Dulcie, handing one to Bess. "Especially after working so hard on Tinker Bell's portrait."

Bess took a bite. "*Mmm*," she said. She closed her eyes and let the flaky layers melt on her tongue. "Delicious,

Dulcie! This is so unexpected – and very nice of you! If there's anything I can do for you, just let me know."

"Well," replied Dulcie, "if you wanted to do a portrait of me, that would be fine! I guess I could even pose for you right now. Why, I could pose with my rolls! What do you think? Should I carry the whole basket or just cradle one in my hand like this?"

Bess swallowed what was left of her roll in one surprised gulp.

"Um… uh… actually," she stammered, "I was just about to… "

"I know!" Dulcie exclaimed. "I'll hold a roll in one hand, and the basket in the other! There! Are you getting this, Bess?"

Bess wiped her buttery hands on her skirt. She hadn't planned to paint another portrait. But how could she refuse? And it certainly was flattering to have such an eager model.

"Okay," Bess said. "Why not? I just need to mix up some paints and pick out my brushes."

Dulcie positively fluttered with glee.

From her box, Bess pulled out jars, each filled with a different colour of paint powder: green, blue, black, gold. She decided to start with the chestnut powder, which was remarkably close to the shade of Dulcie's hair. She poured a small mound onto a piece of glass and added linseed oil. Then she carefully used her palette knife to fold the two together. Soon she had a smooth chocolaty brown paste.

She mixed a few more colours and scooped them onto her palette. Pleased, she pulled a clean paintbrush from her pocket. Then she took a hard look at her model. Bess frowned.

"Dulcie," she said, "I wonder if maybe you could move around a little."

"Move around?" said Dulcie. "But what if I drop my rolls?"

And just then, a knock sounded at the door.

BESS OPENED HER DOOR to find an enormous bouquet of flowers. Two dainty feet in violet-petal shoes poked out below.

"Rosetta? Is that you?" Bess asked.

"Yes, it's me," replied a muffled voice from behind the flowers. Rosetta's pretty face peeked out from the side. "I brought you these," she said. With a groan, she heaved the heavy bunch toward Bess.

"Lily of the valley. My favorite! What a nice surprise, Rosetta!" Bess exclaimed.

Bess managed to drop the flowers into her cockleshell umbrella stand. She knocked over a few paint pots and canvases as she did.

"I thought you'd like them." Rosetta

beamed. "In fact, I thought you might enjoy *painting* them. Or perhaps it would be better for you if I posed *with* them! As if I were walking through my garden, you know? Something like this – "

Pointing her nose in the air, Rosetta rose on one toe and struck a dramatic pose. "Luckily, I just had my hair done. Usually it's such a mess. Make sure you get each curl, now. Oh, this is going to look so great in my room!"

Bess was speechless. "Er… "

"What Bess is trying to say," Dulcie called from across the room, "is that we are already in the middle of a painting." She held up her basket of rolls for Rosetta to see. "As we say in the kitchen, 'First fairy to come, first fairy served!' But don't worry. Bess will let you know when she's done with *my* portrait. Won't you, Bess?"

"Er… ," said Bess.

"Oh, I see," Rosetta said. Her delicate wings slumped sadly. "Well, in the meantime, I'll go clear a space back in my room for my new portrait. I know exactly where it should go!" She gave them both a little wave and hurried out.

"Fly safely!" called Dulcie.

Bess closed the door behind Rosetta. She felt extremely flattered – and still a little stunned. It was part of her role as an art talent to do paintings for her fellow fairies. Till that morning, they had always been for special occasions: an Arrival Day portrait, or a new painting for the Home Tree corridor. In between, she was as free as a bird to paint whatever she wanted.

But now, right out of the blue, *two*

fairies wanted their pictures painted in one day! That was a record for any art-talent fairy, Bess was sure.

Bless my wings, she thought. *Who knew that Never fairies had such great taste!*

"Shall we continue?" asked Dulcie.

Bess picked up her brush and nodded. "Of course!"

But within minutes, another knock sounded at the door… then another… and another!

By midday, fifteen fairies had paid Bess a visit, and fourteen wanted their portraits painted. (Terence, a dust-talent sparrow man, had stopped by only to drop off Bess's daily portion of fairy dust and to compliment her on Tinker Bell's portrait.)

Everyone wanted a portrait just like

Tink's. There were so many requests, in fact, that Bess had given up on painting them one at a time. Instead, she had each fairy come in to sit for a sketch. Her plan was to finish the paintings later. But by the fourteenth fairy, even finishing a sketch began to look iffy.

"Fern, it's really hard to sketch you when you keep dusting my paper," Bess said to the dusting-talent fairy hovering over her easel.

"Oops!" said Fern. She darted back to the pedestal Bess had set up for her. "It's a habit," she explained. "But *really*, Bess." She shook her head. "I do wish you'd let a dusting talent in here once in a while! How can you stand it? And now, with all these baskets and flowers... my goodness! It's a forest of dust-catchers!"

It was true. Bess's studio was even more cluttered than usual. Fairies who'd come hoping for portraits had brought gifts. There were berries and walnuts from the harvest-talent fairies, cheeses from the dairy-talent fairies, and baskets upon baskets of goodies from the talents in the kitchen. Then there were more baskets from the grass-weaving talents. Not to mention a bubbling foot-high fountain from Silvermist, the water-talent fairy.

Luckily, not all fairies had come with gifts. Hairdressing, floor-polishing, and window- and wing-washing fairies had come offering their services. One music-talent fairy even played a song she'd written just for Bess. (To Bess's dismay, it was *still* stuck in her head!)

"Oh!" Fern exclaimed suddenly.

"There's a speck on your pencil there! Hold on!" She examined it. "Looks like pollen." Then another grain caught her eye. "Over there by the door! Fairy dust. I'll bet Terence left that one."

Feather duster waving at full speed, Fern darted about the room. Bess tried her best to sketch the fairy in action.

At least this is the last sketch I have to do, Bess told herself. *Then just fourteen portraits to paint...*

Knock-knock-knock.

Bess's stomach did a backflip. *Again?* For a second, she was tempted to pretend that no one was home. But she quickly realized that Fern's darting glow and humming duster had already given them away.

Slowly, Bess opened the door.

"Oh, Quill! It's you!" Bess let out a sigh of relief that even Fern could hear. "You wouldn't believe how many fairies and sparrow men have come to my studio today," she said.

She tried not to sound boastful. But she wanted Quill to know how much the other fairies liked her work. Bess always felt self-conscious around Quill. Perhaps it was because Quill was so unbelievably neat, while Bess was so messy.

"Fourteen!" Bess blurted, unable to hold back. "Everyone wanting portraits! I've never seen anything like it!" she went on. "I mean, just look at all the things they've brought me!" She waved her brush at the piles of gifts. Then suddenly she paused. "You weren't coming to ask for a portrait, too, were you?"

The art-talent fairy shook her head and smiled. "No, I just came by to see if you were ready to go to lunch. I've heard they're serving mushroom tarts and buttercup soup!"

Buttercup soup! Bess hadn't had that in ages, it seemed. *Mmm* – she could taste it already. Then her eyes fell on the pile of sketches on her table.

"I can't." She sighed. "Everyone is counting on me to finish the portraits as soon as I can. I've never seen fairies so passionate about art." She glanced at Quill out of the corner of her eye. "My portrait of Tinker Bell really touched them. *Deeply!* Mushroom tarts and butter-cup soup will simply have to wait."

Bess sighed again. "It's hard to be so important. But I am up to the challenge – and I won't let Pixie Hollow down! Please give the other art talents my greetings, though, won't you, Quill?"

Quill was about to respond when Fern suddenly poked her head out from behind the birch-bark cabinet.

"Did you say buttercup soup?" she asked. "Hang on, Quill. I'm coming with you!"

She flew across the room, swiping at a few dust grains along the way. "Let me know when my portrait's done, Bess. Oooh! I cannot wait to dust it!" she said brightly.

Bess watched the fairies go, and she shut the door behind them. She looked at the sketch she had *tried* to do of Fern. It wasn't perfect, but it was fine for a sketch, she decided. *And it's probably a good idea to start painting now,* Bess thought. *I have a lot to do!*

Filled with a sense of duty, Bess churned out several portraits in the next few hours. But when she started the portrait of Rosetta, the garden-talent fairy – who had *insisted* on wearing her best rose-petal outfit – Bess froze.

Oh, no!

She couldn't believe it. She was all out of red paint! She couldn't finish Rosetta's portrait without it!

There was just one thing to do: go out and get more. This emergency called for berry juice – and lots of it.

Bess picked up a piece of paper and one of her best calligraphy twigs. She wrote a sign and hung it on her door:

Out to get more paint.
Please come back later.

Bess

Then she grabbed one of Dulcie's rolls, along with the first basket she could find, and flew out into the warm afternoon.

4

THE CURRANT ORCHARD was not far from Bess's studio. It was just across Havendish Stream.

Currant juice was a cheerful bright red, which would make fine paint, Bess knew. As she flew toward the fruits, they looked so pretty that Bess had an urge to paint them right then and there. Ah, but how could she? So many fairies were waiting for their portraits. She couldn't disappoint them.

Bess flitted from branch to branch. She piled as many plump currants into her basket as she could carry. A basketful would be – she hoped – enough for now.

She placed one last fruit atop her wobbly pile, then reached out and picked one for herself. If she couldn't paint the currants, at least she could taste them!

She licked her lips, then took a big hungry bite. The sweet red juice dribbled down her chin. Bess watched it fall, drip by drip, onto her skirt. It mixed with paint splatters there.

She swiped at her chin with the back of her hand. *Yes!* she thought with satisfaction. *This colour will do just fine!*

When she was done eating, Bess grabbed hold of the basket's handle. She stretched up her wings, ready to fly away. The heavy basket, however, was not going anywhere. Bess could pick it up – just barely. But she couldn't carry it more than an inch at a time.

She tried unloading a few currants, but it didn't help much. And if she took out too many, she wouldn't have enough to make paint when she got home.

Enviously, Bess watched a bluebird soaring overhead. If only she could speak to animals like an animal-talent fairy, maybe she could get some help. But she couldn't even tell the gnats hovering around to go away. No matter how hard she shooed, they just kept returning.

"Oh, well," Bess said with a sigh. "I guess an inch at a time will have to do."

Bess flew – or hopped, really – out of the orchard and back toward her studio. By the time she reached Havendish Stream, she had settled into a comfortable rhythm: *flap, flap, flap, flap-jump-land. Flap, flap, flap, flap-jump-land.* But the crystal-clear stream stopped her short.

It wasn't that Havendish Stream was

very big; a young deer could have crossed it in a single leap. To a fairy, however, it was huge. And there wasn't a bridge. Fairies usually just flew over the stream.

What am I going to do now? thought Bess. The stream was too wide to hop across. And though she didn't mind getting her feet and legs wet, she didn't want to risk getting her wings wet, too. Water soaked into fairy wings, as into a sponge. And if the stream was deep enough, waterlogged wings could drag her under.

Still, Bess had gotten this far. She wasn't going to give up now!

She thought for a moment. Then she picked up one of the plump currants. With a mighty heave, she tossed it across the stream. The currant landed with a soft bounce on the moss on the other side.

Bess cheered, then reached for another. Soon she was tossing currants across the stream one after the other.

When her basket was empty, Bess lifted it effortlessly and flew across the stream. Then she refilled it and set off hopping once more. She was quite pleased with her clever solution.

"Now to make some paint!"

Back at her studio, Bess dragged a well-worn coconut shell from its resting place against her crate. She set it on the grass next to the back wall and dumped her basketful of currants into it.

Normally, Bess made her paints in small batches. But she'd spent far more time collecting the currants than she'd planned. If she was ever going to get all those fairies their portraits, she'd have to start speeding things up – a lot! That meant making *lots* of paint.

Bess kicked off her shoes and rolled up her spider-silk leggings. Then, ever so carefully, she climbed into the shell.

"Oops!" Bess slipped and almost fell. She caught herself on the shell.

POP! Squish! The pulpy fruit burst out of its skin and oozed coolly between her toes. Bess stomped around in the bowl. Her feet moved faster and faster.

She tried her best to keep her wings high and dry. But she could tell they were growing heavy with juice. *No matter,* she thought. *They'll have plenty of time to dry while I paint.* She looked down at the ruby red juice in the shell. Her heart filled with joy. Without thinking about it, she began to sing...

"*Oh, fairy, fairy, fly with me –* "

"Bess? What are you doing?"

The voice behind Bess took her by surprise. She wavered, and her foot slipped.

Splash!

Bess fell face-first into the sticky red currant mash.

"Bess?"

Slowly, Bess reached for the edge of the shell and pulled herself up. Peeking over the side, she saw Quill's pretty face staring back. In Quill's hands was a tray full of dishes covered with acorn caps.

"Are you all right?" Quill asked.

"Perfectly fine," said Bess. She spit out a bit of currant. "I'm just – uh – making some paint for all my portraits."

Inwardly, Bess groaned. Why did Quill always catch her in her messiest moment?

With as much dignity as she could manage, Bess pulled herself out of the shell. She tumbled to the ground. Covered in bright red juice, she looked as if she had a very bad sunburn.

"I brought you some dinner," Quill said. She set down the tray. "You need a hot meal to keep up your strength."

Even through the currant juice, Bess could smell the rich scents coming from the dishes. She wished, more than anything, that Quill hadn't seen her this way. But it was hard not to be grateful for such a kind gesture.

"I know I'll enjoy it," Bess said.

"Would you like some help washing

your wings?" Quill asked. Her tone was sincere. But Bess caught the corners of her mouth turning up in a smile.

Bess shook her head and blushed. "Oh, no," she assured Quill. "I'll get to that… when I can."

"As you wish," Quill replied. She fluttered her wings and turned back toward the Home Tree.

5

DESPITE HER EMBARRASSMENT, Bess enjoyed the dinner Quill had brought. And she hoped it would give her more energy to work.

But painting wasn't easy. The currant juice quickly dried into a sticky sap. It made Bess's hair and clothes stiff and her wings all but useless.

If I'm ever going to get more painting done, Bess thought, *I'll have to clean myself up.*

She set off toward Havendish Stream again. Her wings were too stiff now for her even to hop, so instead she walked through the meadow. Unfortunately, because fairies hardly ever walked, there were no paths to follow.

Bess climbed through the grass, in and out of a bush, and through a patch of dandelions. By the time she reached the stream, she could hardly move for all the grass and seeds and fluff sticking to her.

She made her way down the mossy bank to the shore. And then she stopped. How was she going to do this?

Bess knew she should have put aside her pride and let Quill help her wash her wings. It wasn't an easy job for any fairy to do by herself. But at the time, Bess had just wanted Quill to leave.

So now the problem was, what if she fell into the water? She had no idea how deep the water was. But she could see that the stream was running at an impish, happy-to-knock-you-over-and-carry-you-away pace.

Cautiously, she dipped in a toe.

"Ooh!" It was cold!

Still, Bess had little choice. It was much too far to walk back to the Home Tree for a proper bath. So she knelt beside the stream. Cupping her hands, she began to splash water onto herself to try to wash the grass and juice away.

The dried juice in her hair was particularly hard to wash out. Finally, she gave up splashing. She leaned over, ready to stick her whole head in the water.

Crrrooaak!

A frog Bess hadn't noticed leaped into the stream. It landed with a splash. Bess didn't have a chance of keeping her balance. The next thing she knew, she fell headfirst into the water, making quite a splash of her own.

"*Sppplugh!*"

She kicked and waved and sputtered, even though her bottom was firmly on the stream's pebbled floor. Luckily, the water was not very deep. Yet the harder Bess flailed, the faster the playful stream became. At last it began to carry her away!

"Stop! Let me out!" Bess begged.

By then her wings were impossibly heavy. "Help!" Bess cried. "Help! Help! *Help!*"

"Bess!" a voice called out. "Stop kicking! The stream doesn't like it! Just calm down, and I'll pull you out. What were you *doing?*"

Bess made herself relax. A second later, her friend Rani, a water-talent fairy, pulled her out of the water. Bess was safe, if sopping, on a sandy shore.

"Rani, you saved me!" Bess panted, as much with exhaustion as with relief. "You must let me do something for you." She tried to raise herself onto her elbows. But her waterlogged wings felt like weights on her back. She settled for rolling over to face her friend. "I know! How about a – "

" – portrait!" Rani almost shrieked. "Just like Tinker Bell's? Bess, you read our minds! We were just talking about how wonderful it would be for each of us to have a portrait!"

"Each of you?" Bess said, confused.

"Yes, each of us!" Rani replied. "Everyone," she called to a group of water-talent fairies. "Come down here and see Bess. She's going to paint portraits of all of us. We'll be the first talent group to have a complete set!" She teared up with joy. "And could somebody please bring me a leafkerchief?" she asked, sniffing loudly.

In seconds, a dozen eager water fairies surrounded Bess.

"So when can you get started?" Rani asked.

"Well, honestly," Bess began, "I have several others to finish first. And then I'll probably have to make more – "

" – paint!" Rani cut in knowingly. "Of course."

"I hope you'll use *watercolors* for all of our portraits," Silvermist said with a giggle. The whole group of water-talent fairies laughed.

Bess managed to smile politely. She struggled to her feet.

"Oh, here, let me help you," said

Rani. "You'll never get anywhere with wings *that* full of water."

She brushed a bit of fairy dust from her arm onto Bess's wings. Then she held her hands above them. Closing her eyes, Rani drew the water out in a thin silvery ribbon. She formed it into a ball and tossed it into the stream.

"Your wings will still be damp for a while," she said, turning back to Bess. "But at least they won't weigh you down."

Bess stood and gave her wings a little flap. "Much better," she said with relief. But her relief turned to dismay as she thought of the new portraits... a whole *talent*'s worth. Goodness!

As she said good-bye to the water fairies, Bess tried to remind herself that portrait painting was an honour.

"Don't forget about our portraits!" the fairies called after her.

"Oh," said Bess, "I won't."

6

BESS HEADED BACK across the meadow, in the direction of her studio. To her dismay, her flying was a little wobbly since her wings were still a bit damp. *But at least I'm clean,* she thought. She tore off a piece of grass and used it to tie back a lock of hair.

With a sigh, Bess realised that she could use some clean clothes. She hadn't been back to her room in the Home Tree in quite a while. A bit of freshening up in general might do her some good. So she quickly turned away from her studio, toward the Home Tree.

As she neared the knothole door, however, her stomach began to churn. Bess's room was in the tree's south-

southwest branch. That meant passing dozens of rooms and workshops. Who knew how many fairies she might meet along the way? And what if they all wanted portraits? Not that Bess didn't want to paint them all. She just wasn't sure she wanted to do it right *now*.

No, going through the Home Tree was *not* the way to get to her room, Bess decided. She would have to sneak in through her back window instead.

Bess had never flown to her room from behind before. But really, how hard could it be? She circled the trunk to the side where the low evening sun was shining. Thank goodness it hadn't set yet! Then she looked up at the rows of brightly coloured window boxes along the tree's branches.

Now, that's a subject for painting, she thought wistfully. But right now, the window boxes were for counting.

"One… two… three… four… five… "

Bess got to thirteen, but then she had to stop. The Home Tree's leafy branches began to block her view. Bess flew closer and continued counting.

"Fourteen… fifteen… sixteen. Here it is!"

Funny, she thought, *I don't remember that leaf in front of my window.*

Bess flew over to the window and tugged on the sash. Stubbornly, it refused to give. She pulled a little harder. But still the window held fast.

"What am I going to do now?" Bess said. She balled her fists and pounded the window in frustration.

Immediately, the window gave way. Bess tumbled inside.

How odd, she thought, shaking her sore head. *I always thought that window opened out...*

"Bess!" came an alarmed voice from across the room. "Are you all right?"

"Quill!" Bess cried, looking up. "What are you doing here?"

"I'm sculpting – in my room," Quill replied. Her voice now sounded more puzzled than shocked.

"*Your* room?" Bess bit her lip as she rose to her feet. Her eyes darted around the tidy chamber. She looked from one stone sculpture to another, over to the cast-bronze bedstead, and then to the marble busts set into each wall. Finally, her way?" Quill asked again.

"Absolutely not," said Bess. Still grinning, she took a backward hop toward the door… and ran straight into a granite statue of a luna moth. With a crash it fell from its pedestal onto the hard wooden floor.

Bess cringed. "Oh, no!"

"Don't worry." Quill flew over and sprinkled some fairy dust on the heavy statue. Then she used the magic to stand it back up. "No harm done," she said.

"Truly," said Bess, "I'd fly backward if I could."

Quill laughed. "Flying backward is how you knocked it over in the first place."

Bess knew it was a joke. But she couldn't help noticing that Quill hovered eyes went back to Quill.

"Yes," Quill said. "My room. Did you need something, Bess?"

Bess tried to swallow the lump in her throat. She choked out a laugh. "Need something! Ha! That's a good one, Quill. No. No. No. I was just… er… flying by… to let you know I *don't* need anything! And, uh… " She looked down at her limp, wrinkled, stained skirt. "To show you that I cleaned up… all by myself!"

She swallowed once more and stretched her mouth into a grin.

"I see," said Quill. She still looked confused. "I'm… so glad."

"Anyway," Bess went on, "I have portraits of all the water-talent fairies to do. I really must fly off."

"Are you sure I can't help you in some

protectively next to the moth statue.

Bess blushed. "See you later, Quill," she said. And she hurried out of the room before she could do more damage.

Oh, of all the rooms to fall into by mistake, why did it have to be Quill's? Bess thought as she flew to the next room down the hall. She reached for the knob. Then, just to be safe, she checked the number on the door to make sure it was hers.

Inside, Bess's mood quickly lifted. It was a relief to be among her favorite things.

She flew to her bed, which was covered in a multi coloured quilt made from different kinds of flower petals. She lay back and gazed up at the stained-glass window above her. The sun was almost down, but there was just enough light to allow the colours to dance along the wall across the room.

And, oh, the walls! They were covered with framed pictures of every shape and size. Many were gifts from other art fairies. The rest were drawings and paintings that Bess had done herself. There was her very first sketch of Mother Dove. Next to it hung her Home Tree series. She'd followed the tree through all its seasons – spring and summer (which were the only seasons in Never Land).

Each work reminded Bess of a time and place and mood. Some were good and some were bad, but each was special in its own way.

Then her eyes fell on a statue in the corner. It was a portrait of Bess carved out of smooth sandalwood. Quill had given it to her as a gift on her last Arrival Day anniversary. Quill had remembered how much more Bess liked wood than hard, cold stone.

Bess smiled at the statue. It was a perfect likeness, right down to Bess's long bangs and the paintbrush behind her ear.

Funny, Bess thought. She yawned and let her heavy eyelids close for just a moment. *If I didn't know better, I'd say that was the work of a good friend.*

7

THE NEXT THING SHE KNEW, Bess awoke to a loud knock at her door. She didn't even remember falling asleep! What time was it?

Knock-knock-knock.

"Bess! Are you in there?"

Groggily, Bess flew up and opened the door.

"Hi, Bess! It's me! Is it done?"

It was Dulcie.

"I went to your studio. Your sign said you'd be there this morning. But when you never showed up, I thought maybe I'd find you here."

"Oh," said Bess. She pushed her hair out of her eyes, trying to wake up.

"*So?*" Dulcie went on. "Is it done?"

"Is what done?"

"My portrait!"

"Oh!" Bess thought for a moment. "As a matter of fact, it is. But it's not here, of course. It's back at my studio."

"Well, come on!" Dulcie grabbed her arm. "Let's go!"

By the time they reached the tangerine crate, Bess was wide awake. She was pleased to be presenting the new portrait.

She had to admit, though, that she was a little disappointed that Dulcie hadn't brought another plate of rolls, or some other tasty treat.

"I came as soon as I woke up!" Dulcie explained excitedly, almost as if she could read Bess's thoughts. "I haven't even been to the kitchen yet to bake."

"Really?" Bess was touched. How important this was to Dulcie! "Let's take a look, then, shall we?" she said.

She led Dulcie to a row of easels, each draped with a thick velvet-moss cloth. With a quick flick of the wrist, and just the right touch of drama and modesty (something every art fairy arrives with), she yanked off the cover of the nearest one.

"Ooh!" Dulcie fluttered up and down. She clapped her hands. "I love it! I love it!" she gushed. "I can practically taste those poppy puff rolls right now!" And as if to test them, she reached out to touch the painting. Then she stopped.

"What? What is it?" asked Bess.

"Do my wings really stick up like that in back?" Dulcie asked. The joy slowly drained from her face.

"What do you mean?" said Bess.

"My wings!" said Dulcie. "They're… *huge*." She strained her neck, trying to see behind herself. "They're not really that big, are they?"

"Actually, they are," came a cheerful voice from just outside the door. "Good morning, Bess. Dulcie. Is my portrait ready, too?"

"Hello, Rosetta," replied Bess. She was still stunned by Dulcie's reaction. "Er, yes. Yours is done, too."

While Dulcie anxiously compared her wings with those in the painting, Bess reached for the second velvet cover and pulled it off.

Rosetta beamed. Then a tiny wrinkle formed between her brows.

"How do you like the lilies of the valley?" Bess asked. "I tried to make each one practically perfect, just like yours, but not so perfect that they wouldn't look real."

"Oh, yes, they're very nice," Rosetta said. Still, she looked concerned. "It's just … my *nose*. I know for a fact that it's much prettier than *that*."

Dulcie glanced away from her portrait. "Actually, it's not."

Rosetta frowned. "Yes, it is. Would you mind, Bess," she went on, "going back and straightening my nose… and maybe taking a little off the sides?"

"Oh, yes!" said Dulcie. "Could you make my wings smaller, too, Bess? That would be wonderful!"

Bess's mouth fell open. Every fairy had her opinions. But Bess had never before been asked to change her art. Like all talents, she prided herself on doing her best from the very beginning. What were these fairies thinking?

But Bess didn't even have time to reply before a dozen more fairies swooped into her studio, each one eager to see her brand-new portrait. And each one, Bess could tell, was eager to offer her honest opinion.

By the time the fairies had left, Bess was drained – and hungry.

She looked at the sun outside her window. It was high in the sky. She had probably missed breakfast by a good hour. But perhaps a few kind serving talents would still be serving tea.

Bess sure hoped so.

As soon as she reached the Home Tree, she flew straight through the lobby and down the long corridor to the tearoom.

She headed directly for the art-talent fairies' table. As she had feared, the other art-talent fairies had finished their breakfast and returned to their own studios. Most of the tables in the tearoom were empty, in fact. The cleaning-talent fairies were busy taking dirty teacups and breakfast trays away.

"Bessy, dear!" called Laidel, a serving-talent fairy. She swooped up beside Bess. "We were afraid you weren't coming. Let me bring you some tea. And maybe a scone?"

"That would be lovely," said Bess, sinking into a chair.

"Coming right up!" said Laidel.

In moments, the fairy was back. Her

tray was piled high with Bess's favourite tea, sweet cream and clover honey, heart-shaped currant – *Ugh!* Bess thought – scones, blueberry muffins with freshly churned butter, and a tall stack of buckwheat pancakes dripping with warm syrup.

"I thought you looked a bit tired, Bess," said Laidel. "So I brought you a little extra." She gave Bess a wink as she poured a stream of tea into a cup. She set it down before Bess. "Don't tell the other fairies!"

Bess smiled at her gratefully and took a sip. "Ahh! Just what I needed."

"I'm so glad," said Laidel. "Now, just sit back, relax, and enjoy your tea. There you go. I'll come back in a little while and we can talk about my portrait."

Pwahhh! Bess's eyes popped open and the tea she'd been sipping sprayed across the tablecloth. Her cup fell to the floor, where the rest of the tea made a stain on the floral carpet.

Bess reached down to mop it up with her napkin. But another hand, clutching a springy moss sponge, beat her to it.

"Allow me," said Colin, a rather tall (in fairy terms) and rather plump (in any terms) cleaning-talent sparrow man. He dabbed at the spill until no trace of tea was left. Then he flew off with the empty cup and returned in an instant with a new one.

"If there's anything else I can do for you, Bess," he said with a bow, "let me know."

"I will," said Bess.

"For instance," Colin went on, "if you'd like me to pose for one of your portraits, just ask. I'm sure you don't come across a model like *me* every day!"

Bess shook her head. "Er, no, I don't," she said. "But to tell you the truth, Colin, I don't need any more models today. I'm a little behind, I'm afraid."

"No problem," Colin said with a shrug. "We'll do it tomorrow." With a smile, he turned. "Hey, Elda!" he called to a cleaning-talent fairy across the room. "I talked to Bess. She says we should come by her studio *tomorrow!*"

Bess poured a new cup of tea. But the joy of the meal had gone away. Not even the buckwheat pancakes (which had always been Bess's favourite) tasted good.

Maybe I should leave, she thought. *I*

should get busy painting again. Besides, who knows how many more portraits I'll have to do if I stay!

But it was too late. Suddenly, a whole line of eager fairies flew out of the kitchen – baking talents, dish-washing talents, silver-polishing talents, serving talents, and everyone else who happened to be around.

"Hi, Bess," called Dulcie. "Colin said you were here. Did you like the scones? I told everyone in the kitchen about my portrait. And don't you know, now they all want one!"

"Oh, yes!" said another baking-talent fairy. "We've each got to have a portrait, too!"

Bess tried not to groan. But it hardly would have mattered if she had. The fairies were busy chattering with each other, describing *exactly* how they wanted their portraits to be.

"Just be sure to keep your wings tucked in," Dulcie said knowingly.

Finally, Bess held up her hands.

"Friends," she began, "I am truly, truly honoured by your regard for my work. But I'm not sure I can paint all your portraits right now. Maybe a quick sketch would do?" she asked hopefully.

The fairies looked at one another.

"No," said one silver-polisher. "We want *portraits*, like everyone else."

"Yes!" the others chimed in. "We want portraits! We want portraits! We want portraits!"

8

BESS LEFT THE TEAROOM with sixteen more portraits to do.

She hoped she'd have enough paint. But as she pulled one, and then another, paintbrush from the pouch at her waist, she realized she would definitely need more brushes.

Vole hair made the best paintbrushes. Bess could usually find patches of it near the edge of the forest. (Those voles just shed like crazy.) The forest was not far from her studio. She decided that she should fly by and collect some on her way.

And she was so glad she did. The light was *gorgeous*! It was streaming through the trees, casting deep, dark shadows that were so… interesting!

Back to business, Bess reminded herself over and over.

But where were all the vole hairs?

Then, at last, just when Bess thought she would have to make do with dandelion fluff, she spotted a tuft of tiny gray hairs stuck to a blade of grass.

She darted over and began to collect them. All of a sudden, she felt a firm, sharp peck on the top of her head!

"Chrrrp-chrrrp! Trillillillillill!"

Bess spun around to see a stern gray bird staring at her. It was twice as big as she was.

"Eeeek!" shrieked Bess.

"Eeeek!" chirped the bird. *"Chrrr-chrrr-chrrrp-trrrillll!"*

A voice rose from the shadows. "She says she needs those hairs for her nest."

Bess looked to the right and saw a reddish brown head poke out from behind a short stump.

"Fawn," Bess said. "I'd fly backward if I could. I didn't know."

"That's okay," Fawn replied. She was an animal-talent fairy. She could talk to animals in their own languages. "These mockingbirds are a little testy. But they don't mean any harm. Just looking out for their babies."

Bess rubbed the sore spot on her head. "I see." She watched the bird pluck the hairs with her beak.

"Do you think she could spare a few hairs for a new paintbrush?" Bess asked Fawn.

Fawn grinned and turned to the bird. Together, they twittered and chirped for a good three or four minutes. Then the fairy turned back to Bess and nodded.

"Take as many as you need," Fawn said.

"That's kind of her!" said Bess. "What in Never Land did you say?"

Fawn grinned again. "I just told her what a fantastic and famous fairy artist you are. And that you needed hairs for a new paintbrush. *And* that if she shared hers, you would paint her portrait!" She winked at Bess and whispered, "She's quite vain, you know. Oh, and I also told her you would paint me, too."

"Paint you?" said Bess.

"Would you?" asked Fawn. "Everyone is talking about your portraits, and I've never had one done. I just saw Madge's. I don't care how much she thinks she looks like a dragonfly – I think it's wonderful! What a great talent you have! Tell me" – Fawn paused and wrapped her arms fondly around the bird – "do you want to paint us here? Or back at your studio?"

"Right now?" Bess said.

"Why not?" said Fawn with a shrug. "It's early. Besides," she went on with a nod toward the mockingbird, "it's the only way you're going to get your vole hairs."

With a halfhearted sigh, Bess sank onto a patch of moss. She pulled some pencils and her sketchbook from her smock. "I'll *sketch* you here," she told the eager pair. "Then I'll paint you back at my studio. *Alone*."

The mockingbird warbled something

to Fawn. "Be sure to paint her right side – it's her best," Fawn translated. "See, what did I tell you? Oh! And when you do me, don't feel as if you have to make my teeth so big, you know? There are some fairies who call me Chipmunk. Can you believe it?"

Bess began her sketch, just as she'd done for all the fairies.

But she soon found her interest drifting away from her models and off to the forest.

The sun slowly shifted across the late-morning sky. A gentle breeze swept up and blew a flock of woolly clouds across the blue horizon. Closer to the forest's edge, shadows shivered and danced about on the ground.

And then, the west wind kicked in.

At first, it was refreshing. But Never winds are fickle and prone to mischief, especially those from the west. And this one was no different.

It began by blowing all the dandelions' fluff off their stalks, leaving their bald-headed stems to flap about. Then it moved into the trees. It worked the leaves into a rustling frenzy. It sent acorns and hickory nuts crashing to the ground.

Feathers flying, the mockingbird did her best to hold her ground – and her good side. Fawn clung to her neck with all her might.

"Uh, Bess! Shall we call it a day?" Fawn hollered over the din.

"Hold on!" Bess called back. She was sketching furiously in her book. "I'm almost done."

"I *can't* hold on!" Fawn cried.

The mockingbird let out a stream of frantic chirps. The wind gleefully carried away half of them. But Fawn understood.

"She has to get back to her nest, Bess," Fawn shouted. "Crazy wind! Her babies are scared!"

Bess sighed. Fawn was right. They all should go. Besides, by now it wasn't easy to keep her sketchbook from blowing away.

She said good-bye to the mockingbird, who swiftly flew off to her chicks. Fawn asked a chipmunk to carry her and Bess home. And off they rode. Bess held her book of sketches tightly. Her heart was full of newfound joy.

Then the wind died away.

9

BESS COULDN'T WAIT to start painting!

She was bursting with inspiration. Her brushes flew about the canvas.

It wasn't until she stepped back from it that Bess realised that what she had painted wasn't a portrait at all. It was the forest, as she had seen it, in all its pinwheels of texture and color. Great swirls of greens and blues, whites and browns, bright yellows and mysterious grays filled her canvas.

Oh, but it was satisfying! So full of energy and life. Bess hadn't felt this good since she'd finished Tink's portrait. *What's the difference?* she wondered. *What has been missing from all my paintings lately?*

Bess left her studio and flew toward

the Home Tree. On her way, she saw a message-talent fairy. Bess stopped her.

"Do you think you could ask everyone to gather in the courtyard today, just before teatime?" Bess asked her. "The light should be perfect for the unveiling of my newest painting! It's a masterpiece!"

"Of course," the message-talent fairy said, and she quickly flew off.

Bess counted the minutes until teatime. And she couldn't help staring at the masterpiece. Any fairy who appreciated fine painting would absolutely *love* it! She was sure.

Bess's new painting was quite large by fairy standards – five by seven inches. She sprinkled it with fairy dust to make it easier to carry. Then she covered it with a piece of silky cloth and set off for the courtyard of the Home Tree.

Bess had planned on being the first fairy to arrive. But to her surprise, the courtyard was practically full. Everyone was eager to see Bess's great masterpiece.

"It might be a portrait of me!" a dust-talent fairy told a water-talent fairy.

"Or it might be of Fawn," said an animal-talent fairy. "I heard that Bess wouldn't stop sketching her this morning – despite a windstorm!"

"I don't know," someone else said. "It's so large. Perhaps it's *all* of us!"

Finally, it was time. Bess flew up to call everyone to order. Her glow was practically white with excitement.

She smiled at the crowd. "I think you will be glad you flew here today... especially considering what art lovers you all have become! It is because you appreciate art that I couldn't wait to share my newest painting with you. And so… "

Bess grabbed the cloth. She yanked it away with a flourish. "I call it… *Swept Away!*"

In the courtyard, there was silence.

Bess looked happily at her painting. Then she turned to her fans. But the faces staring back at her were blank.

"That's not *me*," she heard one or two fairies mumble.

"That's not me, either," echoed several more.

"No, of course!" Bess chuckled. "It's not any of you. It's… it's a feeling I had of being swept away! In the forest… in the moment… in my art! Isn't it wonderful?"

"It's *what?*" she heard Fawn call out.

"It's a feeling," Bess repeated.

Honestly! Bess's forehead wrinkled in frustration. She began to explain once more – but before she could say another word, the tea chimes rang.

"Teatime!" called Laidel.

"We're coming," several fairies cried in reply.

"Very nice, Bess," said a few water-talent fairies politely as they flew by. Bess looked for tears of emotion. But their eyes were surprisingly dry.

The other art-talent fairies applauded her. But even they seemed more eager than usual to make their way inside.

"Wait!" Bess meekly called. Where were all the adoring fairies? Where were all the requests for paintings of their own? Fiddlesticks! Where were all the compliments Bess had... well... gotten used to?

Within minutes, the courtyard was empty. Bess's glow faded from white to a dull, disappointed mustard color.

She felt her chin begin to tremble. Her eyes welled up with tears.

"Darling, I sincerely hope you're not *crying*. Don't we get enough of that with those pitiful water-talent fairies?"

Bess sniffled and looked up. She saw Vidia flying over.

"I'm not in the mood for your comments right now, Vidia," she managed to say, despite the lump in her throat.

"Suit yourself," said the fairy, turning to go. "I really didn't want to tell you anyway that I liked your painting."

"You *what?*" Bess said with a gasp.

"I like it," replied Vidia, looking back

over her shoulder. "And I'd appreciate it, sweetheart, if you didn't make me say it again."

"Wait!" Bess called out. "Don't go! Stay!" She watched in amazement as the fairy zipped back toward her. "So you really like it?"

Vidia rolled her eyes. "Yes," she said.

Bess grinned. "*Ah*. At least someone does."

"Why, Bess, dear, don't you like it?"

"Well… " Bess stopped to consider Vidia's question. "Yes, I do. I like it very much."

"So there you are. Of course, I can see why you would value *my* opinion. But do you really care so much what those silly slowpokes think?" Vidia scoffed. "Really. And here I thought you were an artist."

It was hard to agree with someone as unpleasant as Vidia. *But she has a point*, Bess thought. Bess loved her painting, and she'd loved painting it. And wasn't that really what art was all about? How could she have let herself forget so easily?

"Um, Vidia," she said. Her hands nervously twisted the cloth that had covered her painting. "Would you, by any chance, like to have this painting?"

For a split second, Vidia actually looked pleased. But her pale face quickly hardened into a scowl. "Darling, are you giving me a present?" she said haughtily. "What in Never Land have I ever done for *you*?"

"You told me the truth," Bess replied. "But more than that, my painting reached you. So I want you to have it."

Vidia's cold eyes moved from Bess to the enormous canvas. And Bess could see them faintly warming.

"I'll take good care of it," Vidia said finally. Then she took a pinch of fairy dust from the pouch hanging from her belt and sprinkled it onto the painting. Picking the painting up, she darted away.

Smiling, Bess watched her go. Then she took a deep breath and braced herself for the difficult task ahead.

10

BESS COULD SMELL the freshly baked honey buns and butter cookies even before she got to the tearoom. But that day, tea would have to wait until after her announcement.

She hated to think about how the other fairies would react. The best thing to do, she told herself, was not think too hard – just do it.

She flew to the front of the great room. She stood between the wide floor-to-ceiling windows and flapped her wings for attention.

"Everyone!" she called. "Everyone! I have an announcement."

The clink of china and the hum of voices, however, did not grow any fainter.

"I *said*," Bess shouted, "I have an

important announcement to make!"

One of her wings accidentally knocked over a tea tray. At last, someone took notice.

"Oh, fairies!" Laidel called out. She clinked a spoon against a cup. "I think Bess has something to say."

The noise died down. All eyes turned to Bess.

"Uh… " Bess was suddenly nervous. How was she going to do this? She wished that she had written her announcement down.

"I… I just wanted to tell you all that I realized something important this morning – something I somehow let myself forget." She brushed her bangs out of her eyes. "The joy of my talent comes not *just* from painting, you see. It comes from painting what *inspires* me, *when* it inspires me. I think that is something you all can understand. I must be true to my talent, and to myself. And so" – Bess drew a deep breath – "although it has been a great honour to be asked to paint so many of your portraits, I won't be able to finish them for quite a while."

Bess closed her eyes. She waited for the backlash.

Clink, clank, slurrrp.

Bess slowly opened one eye, and then the other. All around the room, the fairies had gone back to their tea.

"Wait!" Bess blurted out. "Did you all hear what I said?"

"Oh, yes," several fairies replied.

"We sure did," said a few more.

"You need to be inspired," Laidel

said. "We completely understand."

"I know!" said Dulcie, flying by with a plate of fresh rolls. "Maybe you'd be inspired by Hem's new dress! Stand up, Hem, and show her!"

A plump-cheeked, white-haired fairy modestly stood up. She modelled her frock made of soft pink peony petals. It was tight in the waist and full down to the knees. Hem wore open-toed pink slippers dyed to match. Although Bess liked clothes that were more flowy and colourful, she had to agree that it was very nice.

"Oh, isn't it gorgeous!" cooed Rosetta from the table next to her.

"I've got to have one!" said another garden-talent fairy.

"Me too!" more fairies chimed in.

"Me first, though!" said Dulcie. "Hem promised to make one for me first. Didn't you, Hem? First fairy to come, first fairy served!"

Soon a ring four fairies deep had formed around poor Hem. Teatime – and Bess – had been forgotten.

Bess sank into a nearby chair. She stared, bewildered, at the scene. Could it be that Bess and her portraits had lost all their importance? Had she awakened any real art appreciation in the fairies? Or had her art been just a… just a *fad*?

The idea made her wings limp. Bess's spirits sank. Oh, the horror!

She buried her head in her arms, in case a tear should fall.

"Bess?"

She felt a cool hand on her shoulder.

"Why don't you come to our table?"

Slowly, Bess looked up into Quill's eyes. Her spirits sank even lower. As if making a complete fool of herself weren't bad enough. Did she have to do it right in front of Quill *again?*

"I saved you two star-shaped butter cookies. But if you don't eat them quickly, Linden will."

Bess sniffled a little and shook her head. "I'm not hungry," she said. "I don't know if I'll ever be hungry again."

"Oh, yes, you will," Quill said.

Bess pushed back her bangs. She sniffled once more. "How can you be so sure?"

"Because – " Quill began.

But before she could finish, she was interrupted by Hem's high-pitched voice from the far end of the room. "One at a time, fairies! Please! One at a time!"

Bess and Quill looked over at the ever-widening circle around the dressmaking fairy. They couldn't help smiling at each other.

Quill leaned toward Bess. "Remind me to tell you about the time, a few years before you arrived, when all the fairies decided they just *had* to have their very own tiny hand-carved talent symbols to wear around their necks."

"Really?" Bess was surprised. "That sounds lovely! But... I don't think I've ever seen one."

Quill grinned and nodded. "Exactly."

"*Ah!*" It took a moment, but Bess got it. "Fairies!"

Maybe I will have a cookie or two after

all, Bess thought. And maybe she *would* paint Hem's cute pink dress. Perhaps with a bright green background! Or should it be orange? Or maybe she'd paint something else that day. Or do something with clay? She could even carve with Quill.

There was one thing for sure, though. From then on, whatever Bess did, it would be her choice – and hers alone.

Join Tinker Bell, Prilla and all
the other Never Fairies in
the next Disney Fairies book...

Beck Beyond
the Sea

Here is a fairy-sized preview
of the first chapter!

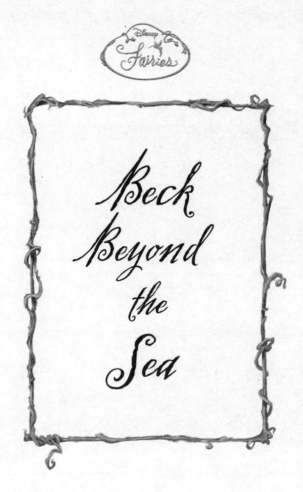

Beck
Beyond
the
Sea

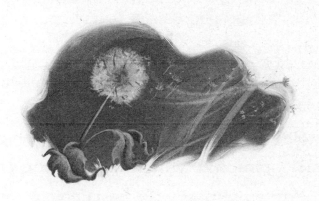

IT WAS A BEAUTIFUL AFTERNOON, cool and clear with a golden glow. Every once in a while, the breeze would puff. It sent dandelion fluff through the air and lifted the tendrils of Beck's hair to tickle her ear.

Beck sighed happily and listened in on a conversation between a pair of chameleons. Beck was an animal-talent fairy, and she could communicate with all the creatures in Never Land. She understood the meaning of every buzz, hiss, peep, coo, growl, purr, bark, and honk.

The chameleons were trying to decide whether they looked better in yellow or orange. Beck was about to offer her opinion – which was that you could never go wrong with basic green – when she spotted a forest boar. She had never seen that boar before. He looked very intent as he trotted along the main path.

Beck flew quietly over him and watched him from above. Where was he going? What was he doing? Was he friend or foe? She followed the boar until he turned off the path and dove under some brush.

Beck flew lower. Where had he gone?

She saw a bush shake. Then a mound of dirt rumbled. Was that him? Yes! Wait! *There* he was. No! There? No!

The boar was gone. He had probably ducked into one of the tunnels below Pixie Hollow. Many years before, the animal-talent fairies had built a maze of underground tunnels that only they could find their way around. Beck hoped the boar wouldn't get lost.

Snort!

The boar popped up from the underbrush. Beck suddenly found herself face to eyeball with him. She was so startled, she somersaulted backward and landed in a sprawl on a broad blade of elephant grass.

The boar made a series of boar sounds. *Snort! Grunt! Snort! Snort! Grunt!*

Snuffle! Snort!

Now, a pots-and-pans-talent fairy, such as Tink, or a water-talent fairy, such as Rani, would have heard a lot of scary boar noises. But remember, Beck was an animal-talent fairy. Even though she had never met this boar before, she knew what the noise was – good-natured laughter. The boar was not an enemy.

Beck sat up, straightened her tunic, and flew closer. The boar snuffled a bit, but Beck understood him perfectly. "Aha! Caught you," he said. "You're following me, aren't you?"

"Yes," Beck answered. "Are you angry? I know spying is bad manners."

"I'm not angry. But why are you following me? Have I done something wrong?"

"No, no, no!" Beck answered. "I was just curious. Whenever I see strangers, I wonder where they came from and where they are going."

The boar lifted his hairy upper lip to show a set of long, sharp white teeth.

Another fairy might have mistaken this for a menacing snarl. But Beck saw a friendly smile. The boar told her, "I'm from the eastern tip of Never Land, and I'm on my way to the western side of the Never Land forest. There are truffles there that taste like clouds dipped in joy. And when the rain falls, it makes a noise like nothing you've ever heard. It's just like music. You can settle under a rotten log and listen all afternoon. Here's the song I heard on my last visit."

He threw back his head and began to

sing in his snuffly boarlike way. *Snuffle Snuffle Snort Snort Grunt Grunt Snoooooorrrrt!*

Beck felt chills up and down her spine. Even through his snorts and snuffles, she could hear the music plainly. It was a strange, beautiful melody.

When he was done, she clapped. "The rain never makes music like that in Pixie Hollow," she said. "I wonder why."

"Different plants. Different dirt. Different sound," the boar explained. "It's a beautiful place, Pixie Hollow, but you just don't get the music here that you get in the western forest. Or the truffles, either."

Beck sighed. "I wish I could hear a rain song."

"Come with me," he invited. "It

takes only a few weeks to get there."

Beck shook her head sadly. "In Pixie Hollow, there's just enough of everything. No more, no less. Every fairy gets one teacup of fairy dust a day. My dust wouldn't take me that far. Without it, I can't fly."

"Well, you can walk. And when you get tired, you can ride on my back."

Beck was touched. That was a very nice offer. "I wish I could. But I can't. If I left, who would take care of Mother Dove?"

"I've heard of her. Wonderful bird. Love to meet her sometime. Not today, though. I've got to get going before the truffle season is over." He twitched an ear. "Good-bye."

"Good-bye," Beck said as the boar

turned and trotted off.

She was still watching him when she heard a heavy rustle above her. She looked up. A flock of strange blue-and-yellow-striped birds passed overhead.

Those birds fascinated Beck. They always flew fast and stayed in a perfect star formation that turned in the sky like a pinwheel.

But they never stopped to visit. They moved right past Pixie Hollow. What kind of birds were they? Where were they going? As she watched, they passed over the treetops and soared into the distant sky.